GREAT ORG
TRANSCRIPTIONS

26 Works by Liszt, Saint-Saëns, Bach and Others

Selected and with an Introduction by
ROLLIN SMITH

DOVER PUBLICATIONS, INC.
Mineola, New York

Bibliographical Note

This Dover edition, first published in 2005, is a new compilation of works originally published separately in authoritative early editions. We are indebted to organist/author Rollin Smith for providing scores and an introduction prepared especially for this edition.

International Standard Book Number: 0-486-44163-6

Manufactured in the United States of America
Dover Publications, Inc., 31 East 2nd Street, Mineola, N.Y. 11501

INTRODUCTION

Now that playing organ transcriptions has come back into vogue, we present this collection of 26 arrangements from the scores of the great masters—to use the title of the series published in the late 19th century by the great W.T. Best, one of the most prolific organ transcribers. It is as true today as it was in 1892 when Best wrote that an arrangement of "a well-known instrumental adagio or andante is infinitely preferable to the frequently dull specimens of modern organ music duly vaunted as being 'original.'" Indeed, organists today feel, as did many of those great players of the past century, that transcriptions are played not with the idea that the organ is an orchestra, or that it is intended to imitate one, but in the belief that great music transcends its medium of expression. Included in this volume are some true masterpieces of the transcriber's art. R.S.

JOHANN SEBASTIAN BACH
SINFONIA TO CANTATA NO. 29, *WE THANK THEE, GOD*

This overture, in the spirit of the cantata, is an extended and jubilant fanfare. It received its first performance on August 27, 1731, in connection with civic festivities at the Town Hall of Leipzig. Bach transcribed this work for organ, strings, trumpets, oboes, and timpani, from the third movement of his Partita in E for solo violin. The great French organist, Alexandre Guilmant (1837–1911) included this Sinfonia in the third volume of his *Répertoire des Concerts du Trocadéro*.

CHACONNE, BWV 1004

A chaconne is a continuous theme and variations in which a short subject is repeated and varied either as a melodic bass or as a harmonic progression. In the *Chaconne*, from the second Partita in D Minor for violin solo, Bach varies his four-measure theme for nearly fifteen minutes. Johannes Brahms, in a letter to Clara Schumann, wrote, "To me the *Chaconne* is one of the most beautiful, incredible compositions. On one staff, and for a small instrument, this man pours out a world full of the most profound thoughts and most powerful emotions."

Bach's *Chaconne* has been transcribed, arranged, and had accompaniments written for it more than for any of his other works. These range from piano accompaniments (Mendelssohn and Schumann), orchestral accompaniments, arrangements for piano left hand (Brahms), piano solo (Busoni's being the most famous), and from string quartet, chamber ensembles, and string orchestra, to full orchestra, as well as at least four versions for organ solo.

Wilhelm Middelschulte (1863–1943), a German organist and composer who settled in Chicago in 1891 and was noted for his performances of Bach's organ works, was inspired by Busoni's concert arrangement for piano (premiered in Boston in 1893) and in 1912 published his own arrangement. He believed, as Busoni stated, that an arrangement was "justified by the significant content that is not expressed sufficiently by the violin, and because of the example of Bach's own transcription of his Violin Fugue in G Minor, BWV 539."

We are grateful to Brink Bush, a noted Middelschulte specialist, who provided a copy of this rare score.

SICILIENNE

A movement from Bach's Sonata for flute and clavier, BWV 1031, this was arranged by Louis Vierne (1870–1937) while he was a student of and assistant to Charles-Marie Widor, organist of Saint-Sulpice, Paris. It was published in 1894, (the year Vierne won a first prize in Widor's organ class at the Paris Conservatoire) in the third volume of *L'Orgue Moderne*—a quarterly series edited by Widor. It is curious that, since the solo was composed for a flute, Vierne registers it for the clarinet.

JOHANNES BRAHMS
HUNGARIAN DANCE NO. 5

In 1850 the Hungarian violinist Eduard Reményi introduced Brahms to the music of the Hungarian Gypsies. Brahms later composed 21 Hungarian Dances based on traditional Gypsy melodies for piano duet. The most popular is the fifth in F-sharp minor published in 1869, in which Brahms penetrated deeply the Hungarian spirit, caught color, swing, perfume, mad melancholy, and reckless joy.

FRÉDÉRIC CHOPIN
PRÉLUDE, OP. 28, NO. 4

Chopin's Prelude in E Minor was arranged in 1864 to be included in Alexander Gottschalg's *Repertorium für Orgel, Harmonium oder Pedalflügel* "under the editorship and with contributions by Franz Liszt." While it has been documented that the greatest pianist of the 19th century did not play the organ very well—he seems always to have improvised or had someone else play the pedal part—Liszt certainly knew how to transcribe for the instrument.

Since this transcription was published in Germany, Chopin's terms were translated into German (*Klagend:* espressivo; *Sehr ruhig und gebunden* (very calm and legato). Liszt's phrasing differs from Chopin's: he prefers two-note groupings whereas Chopin sometimes phrased ten measures together; in measure 19 Liszt omits the acciaccatúra on the fourth beat; and he omits all dynamic indications except the *pianissimo* in the penultimate measure.

This Prelude was played at Chopin's funeral; one but wonders if the performance was from Liszt's arrangement.

FRANÇOIS COUPERIN
SŒUR MONIQUE

The Rondeau *Sœur Monique* is one of Couperin's many harpsichord pieces. From the Third Book (XVIII Order), it is an aural portrait of a nun, Sister Monica. Originally transcribed for organ by Alexandre Guilmant, it was one of the staples of his recital programs as well as that of his students Joseph Bonnet and Marcel Dupré. The eminent American organist, Lynnwood Farnam (1885–1930), published his own transcription in 1920.

CLAUDE DEBUSSY
PRELUDE TO *THE BLESSED DAMOZEL*

In 1884 Debussy won the Grand Prix de Rome, a prize given by the Académie des Beaux-Arts, that allowed successful candidates to become pensioners of the government for four years. The time is spent in Rome at the Villa Medici where the winner composes and from time to time sends back new works. Debussy sent a setting of a French translation of

Dante Gabriel Rosetti's *The Blessed Damozel,* a cantata, or *poème lyrique,* for female voices (chorus and solo) and orchestra. The judges considered its modern tendencies too extreme and denied it the customary public performance.

Palmer Christian (1890–1947), who transcribed this work, was for 23 years organist at the University of Michigan and retired as head of the organ department. In 1920, when he published this, one of his few transcription, he was the municipal organist of Denver, Colorado.

CHARLES GOUNOD
FUNERAL MARCH OF A MARIONNETTE

Known to a generation of television viewers as the theme music for Alfred Hitchcock's mystery program, this popular trifle was composed for a ballet included in the incidental music for Jules Barbier's drama *Jeanne d'Arc,* premiered in Paris on November 8, 1873. It became so popular in England that within two years it had earned Gounod at least £350. This arrangement is by the great English organ virtuoso W.T. Best (1826–1897) and typically includes the orchestration in small type.

GEORGE FRIDERIC HANDEL
HALLELUJAH CHORUS

The Hallelujah Chorus from *Messiah* has remained one of Handel's most beloved works. At its first performance the audience "was so transported that they all, with King George II, who was present, started at once to their feet, and remained standing till the Chorus ended." This tremendous music has lost none of its effectiveness and during public performances today the same reverence is paid.

LARGO FROM *XERXES*

The celebrated *Largo* is an aria from Handel's opera in which Xerxes expresses his gratitude for a garden tree whose branches shade him from the heat of the sun. It has been arranged for organ more than any other work. This transcription was made by Edwin Arthur Kraft (1883–1962), organist of Trinity Cathedral in Cleveland for 50 years.

THE HARMONIOUS BLACKSMITH

This set of five variations is from the *Suite in E* in the first volume of Handel's harpsichord pieces published in London in 1720. Its popular title, "The Harmonious Blacksmith," is derived from an anecdote invented after Handel's death that described the composer's taking shelter during a storm at the smithy of a man named Powell. The blacksmith, in the midst of his work, was singing a tune to the accompaniment of his anvil. Handel, enchanted, took both the tune and the accompaniment for his own. Wanda Landowska wrote that "I regret to say, at the risk of disillusioning the legend-loving devotees of the *Harmonious Blacksmith,* that it is neither Harmonious nor Blacksmith, but simply an *Air* with *Doubles,* which means with variations." The German organist/composer Sigfrid Karg-Elert (1877–1933) published this concert arrangement for organ in 1913.

FRANZ LISZT
SAINT FRANCIS OF ASSISI PREACHING TO THE BIRDS

There is a legend that St. Francis, a friend of all God's creatures, preached to his brothers the birds and they joined in prayer with him by singing. This tone poem, one of two *Légendes,* is dedicated to Liszt's daughter Cosima, later the wife of Richard Wagner, and was published in 1866 simultaneously in Paris and Budapest.

This *Légend* was a favorite of Camille Saint-Saëns (1835–1921) and he included it in the organ recital he played at the Trocadéro in September 1878. Liszt was delighted with the effect of his piece on the organ and wrote Saint-Saëns:

> I am still quite awestruck at your *Prédication aux oiseaux.* You use your organ as an orchestra in an incredible way, as only a great composer and a great performer like yourself could. The most proficient organists in all countries have only to take off their hats to you.

Evidently, Saint-Saëns played it frequently when he was organist of La Madeleine because the priests accused him of making their instrument sound like a "bird organ!"

It was also the subject of one of his most-frequently told anecdotes:

> . . . after I had played the delightful *Saint Francis of Assisi Preaching to the Birds* of Liszt at a wedding, the officiating priest called me into the sacristy to tell me that it sounded as if I were tuning the organ and that if I went on that way they would engage another organist.
>
> "I will go whenever it may be desired," was my answer.
> But I did not go until I myself desired.

JULES MASSENET
ANGÉLUS

Known mainly as opera composer, Massenet composed seven orchestral suites. *L'Angélus* is from the fourth suite, *Scènes pittoresqus,* first performed in 1874. The *Angélus* is a dream piece for organists: it has melody, chimes, harp, and a brief chorale section, all skillfully alternated and combined.

NICOLAS-JEAN, LE FROID DE MÉREAUX
TOCCATA FROM *ŒDIPE ET JOCASTE*

The Parisian composer, Nicolas-Jean Le Froid de Méreaux (1745–1797), known for two oratorios and nine operas, was organist of Saint-Sauveur, the Church of the Petits Augustins, and the Chapelle Royale. The Toccata from his 1791 opera, *Œdipe et Jocaste,* based on Sophocles play, was arranged for organ by Clarence Dickinson (1873–1969) and published in 1909 by Clayton F. Summy in Chicago— just as Dickinson was leaving for New York to become organist of the Brick Presbyterian Church.

GIOACCHINO ROSSINI
OVERTURE TO *WILLIAM TELL*

Guillaume Tell was the masterpiece with which Rossini closed his operatic career at the age of 37. The Overture moves from a serene Alpine landscape through a storm after which peace again prevails. The scene changes to a spirit of martial energy and instead of the piping of the cow herders the call to arms is heard. It ends is in a jubilant mood of victory.

This transcription by Dudley Buck (1839–1909), one of America's early organ virtuosos and popular church music composers, was published in 1868 and remained a favorite with recitalists until well into the 20th century.

ANTON RUBINSTEIN
RÊVE ANGELIQUE, Op. 10, No. 22

Kamennoi-Ostrow (Stone Island) is one of a group of islands in the Neva River on which was a pleasure resort for the residents of St. Petersburg. Rubinstein lived there for a while and made his stay famous by composing a group of 24 portraits descriptive of scenes, incidents, or persons on the island. *Rêve angelique* is a musical portrait of Mlle. Anna de Friedebourg, one of the composer's friends.

CAMILLE SAINT-SAËNS
The Nightingale and the Rose

A drama in three acts, *Parysatis* was premiered at Béziers on August 17 and 19, 1902. Its ostentatious instrumentation consisted of an orchestra of 450 instruments, including 20 harps, and a chorus of 250. The text was by Jane Dieulafoy, an archeologist who discovered Susa, the ancient capital of the kings of Persia—a find so important that she received the Cross of the Légion d'Honneur.

Parysatis, the queen and half-sister of Darius II (*d.* 404 B.C.), was an influential but cruel woman who wielded much influence over her husband, in particular by having their 16-year-old son Cyrus appointed commander of the Persian army in Asia Minor.

The most famous excerpt from *Parysatis* is the soprano aria, *Le Rossignol et la Rose,* a wordless vocalize, the trills and roulades of which were notated by Saint-Saëns at a Greek café in Alexandria and which he often inscribed on concert programs. Originally transcribed for organ by Louis Courtade, organist of Toulouse Cathedral, it was played so often by Clarence Dickinson that he eventually owned three copies, each covered with registration written in colored pencil. The present score incorporates Dr. Dickinson's registration with that of M. Courtade's. Also included are the improvised melismas (between Vi–de) added by Mabel Garrison (1886–1963) on her Victor acoustic recording.

The Swan

The Carnival of the Animals, a "grande fantaisie zoologique," is a set of 14 humorous pieces for chamber orchestra each of which describes a particular animal, usually by mimicking the sound it makes or by characterizing the way it moves. *The Swan* was the only movement Saint-Saëns allowed to be plublished in his lifetime (the ban was lifted in his will) and there are few instruments for which it has not been arranged. Originally for cello and piano, its warm expressiveness has been seen to evoke the graceful contours of the swan's neck or the grace with which it glides through the water.

ROBERT SCHUMANN
Abendlied, Op. 85, No. 12

Originally a piano piece for three hands, the *primo* playing a single line, *Abendlied* is one of 12 piano pieces for four hands written for "kleine und grosse Kinder." Schumann's *Evening Song* has appeared in numerous arrangements for organ as well as for many other instruments.

PETER ILYITCH TCHAIKOVSKY
Three Danses caracteristiques

These three *Danses caracteristiques* from the ballet *The Nutcracker,* display Tchaikovsky's originality and keen fancy for effects, particularly for unique orchestration. First performed in St. Petersburg in March 1892, *The Dance of the Sugar-Plum Fairy* was the first major work to use Victor Mustel's newly-invented Celesta. All three dances were transcribed by

Gordon Balch Nevin (1892–1943), a well-known Cleveland organist and composer.

Danse Arabe was a favorite of Leopold Stokowski when he was organist of Saint Bartholomew's Church in New York (1905–8) and when he played it during a church service he listed it as "Mélodie Arabe."

ANTONIO VIVALDI
Largo e spiccato

Long thought to be an organ concerto by Wilhelm Friedemann Bach with the manuscript in the hand of his father, it was discovered in 1911 to be Vivaldi's Concerto Grosso, Op. 3, No. 11, for two violins, cello, string orchestra, and continuo. The second movement is a siciliano. Since the compass of Bach's organ at Weimar did not extend to high D, he wrote the second to last right hand notes in measures four and 12 as an A. You might want to follow Vivaldi's original and play octave Ds for the last two beats in these measures.

RICHARD WAGNER
Liebestod from *Tristan und Isolde*

In the bleak courtyard of Tristan's crumbling castle, the wounded hero rests on a couch. As Isolde's ship arrives, Tristan, ecstatic in his eagerness to see her, runs to meet her, clutching at the bandages that are swathed about his wound, bleeds to death and sinks a corpse at his beloved's feet. Isolde tries to call her lover to life and, failing, she sings this death song and falls lifeless across Tristan's body.

Published in 1902, this arrangement is by Archer Gibson (1875–1952), then organist of New York's Brick Church. He devoted the rest of his life to playing the organs in the homes of the wealthy. Among his patrons were Henry Clay Frick, Charles Schwab, John D. Rockefeller, Louis Comfort Tiffany, and many others.

Pilgrim's Chorus from *Tannhäuser*

Franz Liszt made three versions of the Pilgrims Chorus from Wagner's *Tannhäuser:* one for piano in 1861; and two for organ, the first in 1860, and the present arrangement that dates from 1862. Both organ arrangements include an optional second ending composed by Liszt. It is the setting of the chorus of old pilgrims from the first scene of Act III, transposed from the key of E-flat to E Major, and Liszt included the beginning of the text, "Der Gnade Heil."

Introduction to Act III and Bridal Chorus
from *Lohengrin*

The brilliant and impressive prelude depicts the happiness at the wedding festivities of Elsa and Lohengrin. Exalted and jubilant themes paint a scene of royal pageantry.

The Bridal Chorus is heard as the curtain rises on the third act. The scene is the bridal chamber of Elsa and Lohengrin and, as the king, nobles, ladies, and pages enter, the chorus sings:

> Faithful and true, we lead ye forth,
> Where love triumphant shall crown ye with joy!
> Star of renown, flow'r of the earth,
> Blest be ye both from all life's annoy.

CONTENTS

SŒUR MONIQUE

RONDO

Swell : Oboe
Great : Flute 8'
Choir : 8' and 4'
Pedal : 16' and 8'

FRANÇOIS COUPERIN
1668–1733

Arranged by Lynnwood Farnam

Piccolo off
add Oboe

sempre staccato

repeat
pp

LARGO E SPICCATO

from Concerto Grosso, Op. 3, No. 11

Transcribed by Johann Sebastian Bach

ANTONIO VIVALDI
1678–1741

Manuals

Pedal

HALLELUJAH CHORUS

from *Messiah*

GRAND CHŒUR sans plein jeu ni Anches de 16 pieds
Réserver quelques jeux de fonds et le plein jeu pour la fin
Claviers accouplés — Tirasses

FULL ORGAN with neither loud mixtures nor 16' reeds
Reserve some foundation stops and the mixtures for the end
Manuals coupled — All manuals coupled to Pedal

GEORGE FRIDERIC HANDEL
1685–1759

Transcribed by Théodore Dubois

★ Au deux endroits marqués de ce signe, la partition chant et orchestre contient deux mesures de plus, que nous avons cru devoir supprimer dans cette transcription, pour éviter la monotonie qui résulte de leur exécution sur l'orgue.

★ At the two places indicated by this sign the full score contains two more measures. We think they should be cut in this transcription in order to avoid the monotony that results from their performance on the organ.

14

LARGO

from *Xerxes*

Sw. Voix Celeste, Oboe & Tremolo
Gt. Diapasons 8ft. Bourdon 16 ft. uncoupled
Ch. Concert Flute 8 ft.
Ped. Diapason 16 ft. coupled to Gt. and Ch.

GEORGE FRIDERIC HANDEL
1685–1759

Transcribed by Edwin Arthur Kraft

Most respectively dedicated to Paul Faust-Barmen, organ builder

THE HARMONIOUS BLACKSMITH

Variations in E Major

Concert Arrangement by Sigfrid Karg-Elert

GEORGE FRIDERIC HANDEL
1685–1759

Var. I. Un poco più animato

Var. II. Poco tranquillamente

Var. III. Allegro molto veloce

Var. IV. Pochettino tranquillo (non slentando!)

* *8va* only if 16' foundation stops are included.

24

Var. V. Allegro risoluto

SINFONIA FROM CANTATA NO. 29

Wir danken dir, Gott, wir danken dir

Grand-Chœur sans 16 P. à tous les claviers.

Pos. ou Récit accouplé au Gd.-O.

PÉDALE: Fonds de 16, 8 et 4 P. (Anches préparés).

Tirasse du Récit et du Pos.

JOHANN SEBASTIAN BACH
1685–1750

Arranged by Alexandre Guilmant

(*) Ces petites notes ne doivent servir que pour les pédaliers
ne montant que jusqu'au Ré.

(*) These small notes ought to be played only upon Pedals
which do not go above D.

CHACONNE

from *Sonata (Partita) No. 2 in D Minor* for solo violin, BWV 1004

Arranged by Wilhelm Middelschulte

JOHANN SEBASTIAN BACH
1685–1750

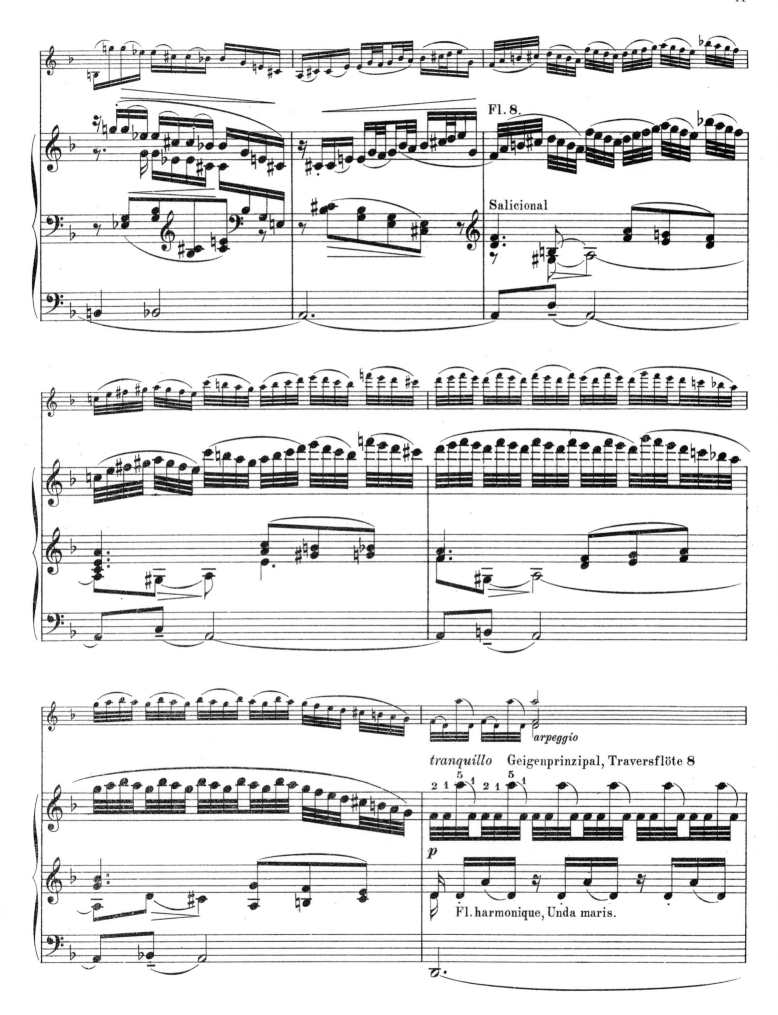

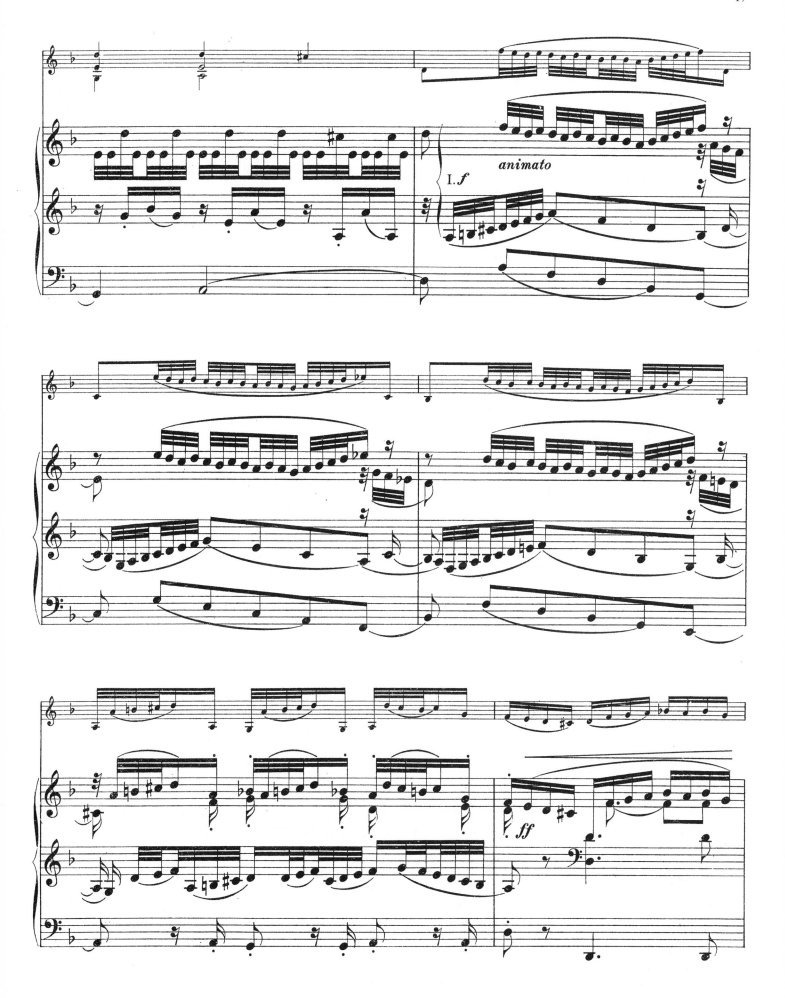

55

SICILIENNE

from *Sonata in E-flat,* BWV 1031

G. Flute 8.
P. Bourdon 8. (ou Flûte 8.)
R. Clarinette.
Péd. Flûte 8.

Arranged by Louis Vierne

JOHANN SEBASTIAN BACH
1685–1750

TOCCATA

from *Œdipe et Jocaste*

Sw. 8' & 4' Flute stops
Gt. Doppel Flute & Gamba
Ch. Melodia & Piccolo
Ped. Bourdon 16', Swell to Pedal

Arranged by Clarence Dickinson

NICOLAS-JEAN LE FROID DE MÉREAUX
1745–1797

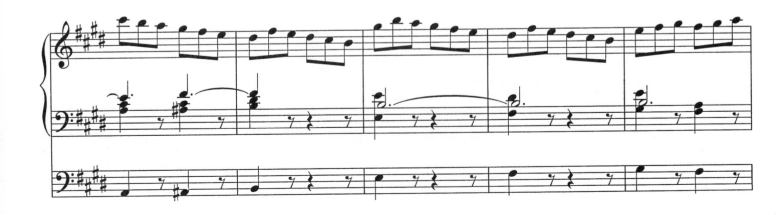

64

PRÉLUDE

Op. 28, No. 4

Arranged by Franz Liszt

FRÉDÉRIC CHOPIN
1810–1849

OVERTURE TO *WILLIAM TELL*

Transcribed by Dudley Buck

GIOACCHINO ROSSINI
1792–1868

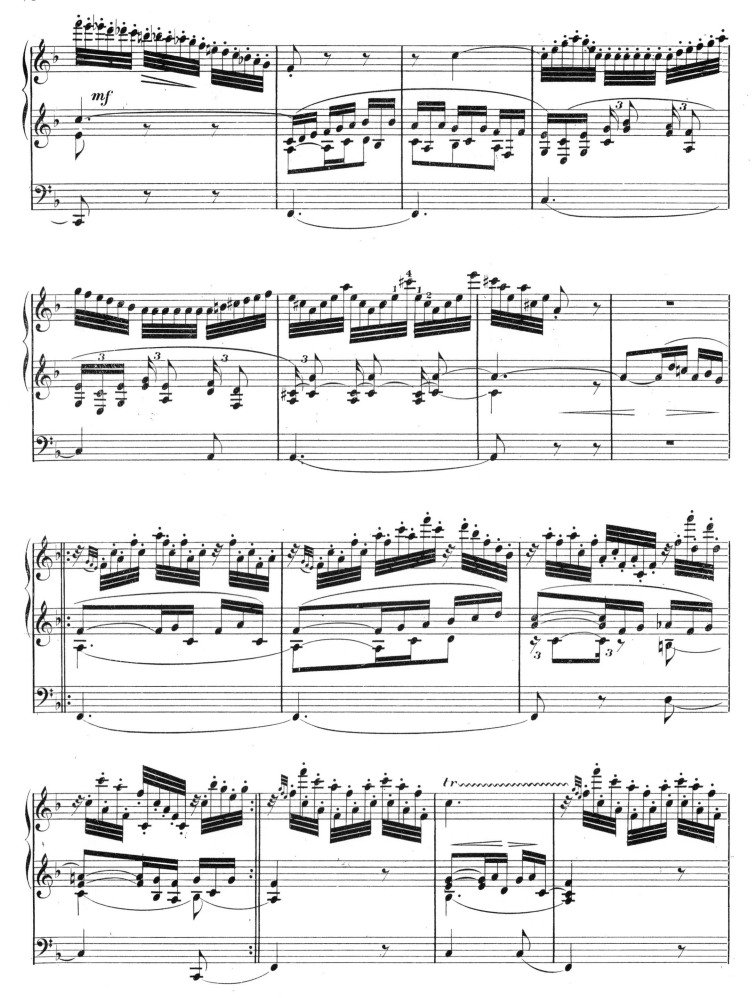

to Frau Eduard Bendemann

ABENDLIED
Op. 85, No. 12

ROBERT SCHUMANN
1810-1856

Arranged by Sigfrid Karg-Elert

Ausdrucksvoll und sehr gehalten.

LIEBESTOD

(Love-death)

from *Tristan und Isolde*

S   Soft String Stops, with Vox Celestis, Viol d'Orchestre, & Tremolo
G   Flute 8' coupled S & C
C   Soft 8' Concert Flute, and Dolce, coupled S
P   To suit comb. in use, and always coupled to Sw.

RICHARD WAGNER
1813–1883

Transcribed by Archer Gibson

suddenly remain
pp *pp* *pp*

repeat <u>all</u>
notes not <u>tied</u>

(close Swell
Boxes tight,
suddenly)

cresc. _ - - -

cresc. molto

f

(N.B. *Not ff*, but only *f*;
avoid heavy stops; use only
such as blend naturally
with those already drawn.)

★ Thumb of right hand on **GSC** should play lowest note of right hand part to end. If the fingers be too short, play on one manual.

PILGRIM'S CHORUS

from *Tannhäuser*

RICHARD WAGNER
(1813-1883)

Transcribed by Franz Liszt

*) Anstatt der nachfolgenden 23 Takte können folgende 5 Takte als Schluss gebraucht werden.

*) The following 23 measures can be cut and replaced by Liszt's five measure original ending.

INTRODUCTION TO ACT III
AND BRIDAL CHORUS

from *Lohengrin*

GRAND-CHŒUR sans Anches de 16 p. ni plein jeu
Claviers accouplés
PÉD. tous les fonds. Tirasse Positif et G.-Orgue
    Anches préparées.

RICHARD WAGNER
1813–1883

Transcribed by Théodore Dubois

à Mlle. Anna de Friedebourg

RÊVE ANGÉLIQUE

from *Kamennoi-Ostrow,* Op. 10, No. 22

III. Swell soft 8 & 4 ft.
II. Great Wald Flute 8 ft.
I. Choir Lieblich 8 ft.

ANTON RUBINSTEIN
1829–1894

Transcribed by Edwin H. Lemare

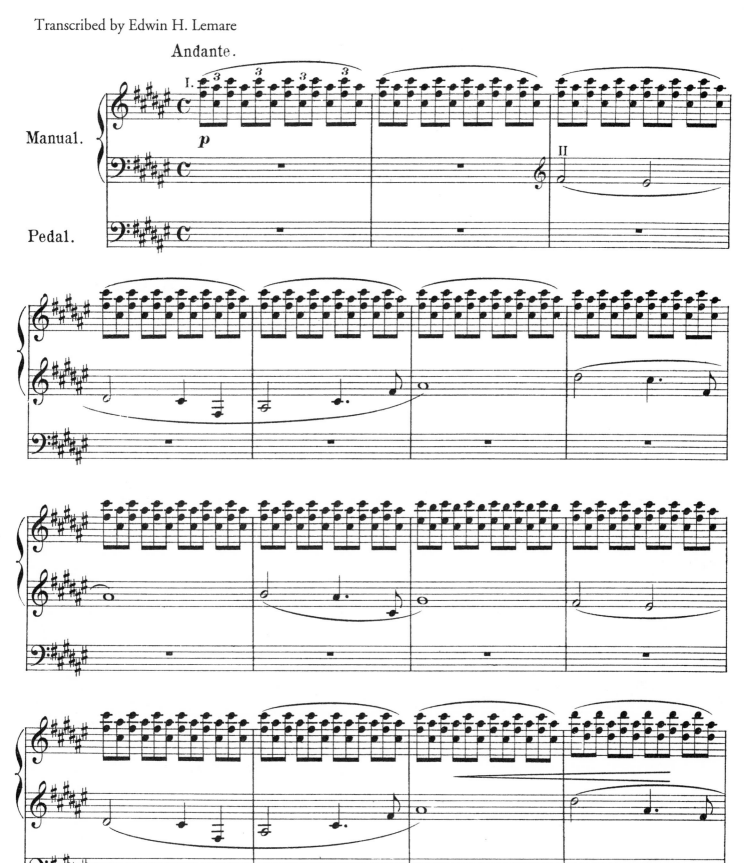

ST. FRANCIS OF ASSISI PREACHING TO THE BIRDS

St. François d'Assise. La Prédication aux oiseaux.

(Die Vogelpredigt)

Arranged by Camille Saint-Saëns

FRANZ LISZT
1811–1886

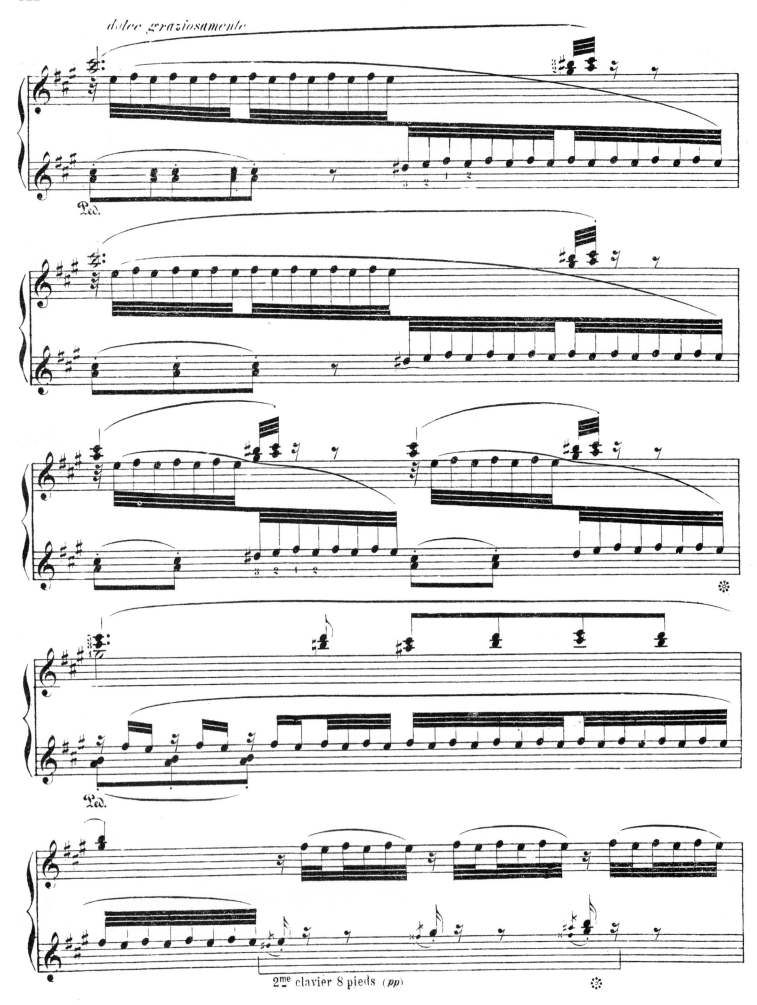

2ᵐᵉ clavier

sempre dolce

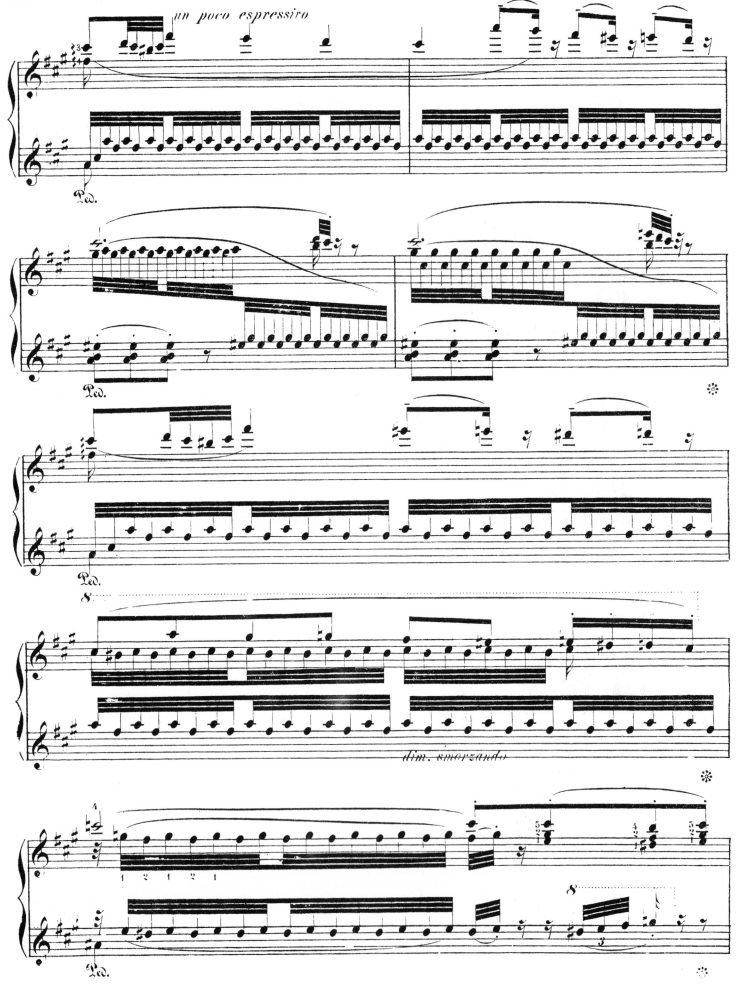

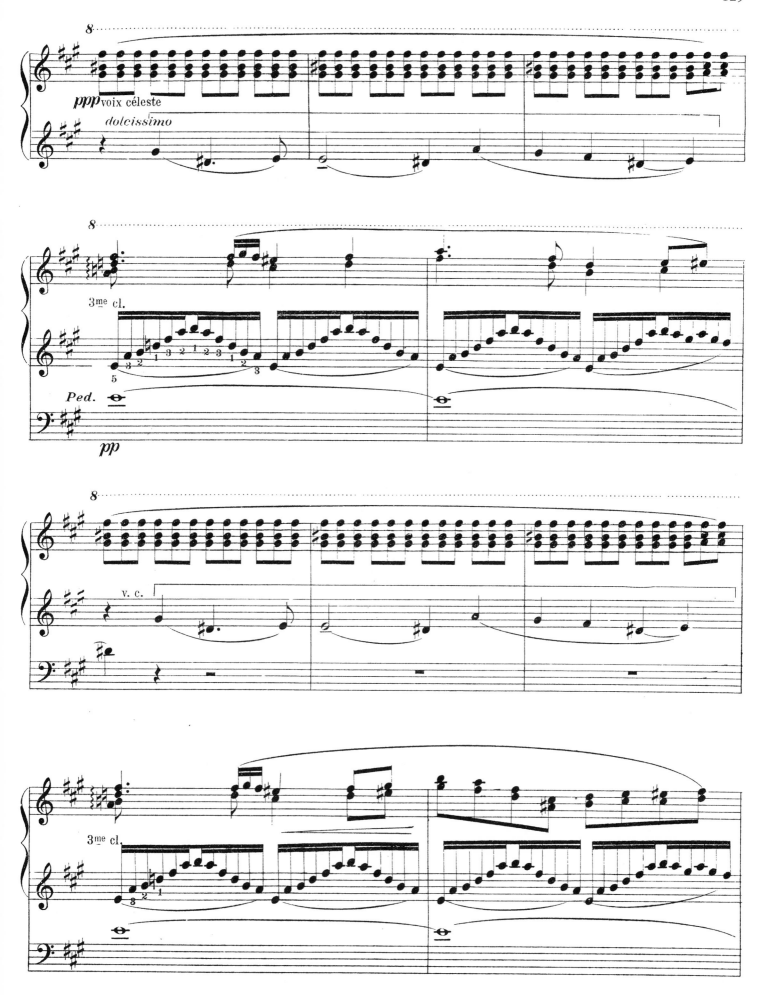

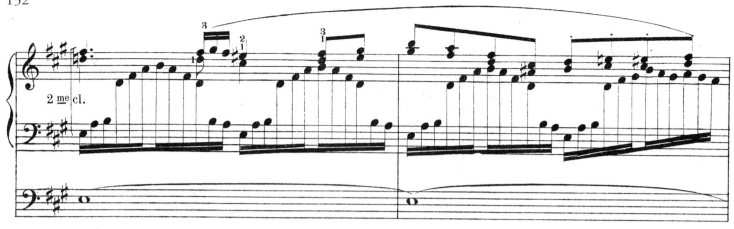

2 <u>me</u> cl.

poco a poco cresc. ed accel.

2<u>me</u> cl.

1<u>er</u> cl.

(8 et 16 p.)

HUNGARIAN DANCE NO. 5

Arranged by Edwin H. Lemare

JOHANNES BRAHMS
1833–1897

THE FUNERAL MARCH OF A MARIONETTE

l'Entrerement d'une Marionnette

from *Jeanne d'Arc*

Swell. Full
Great. Full to Mixtures
Choir. Clarinet and Flute 8'
Pedal. 16' & 8' (couplers ad lib.)

CHARLES GOUNOD
1818–1893

Arranged by W.T. Best

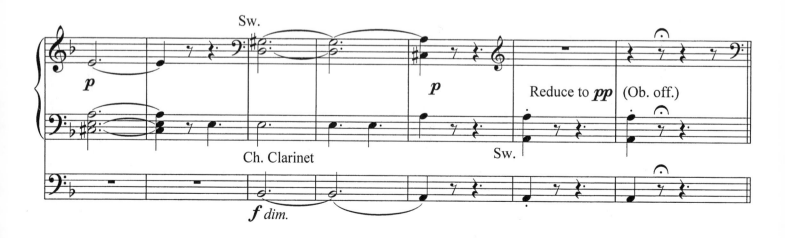

Hommage à Madame JANE DIEULAFOY

THE NIGHTINGALE AND THE ROSE

from *Parysatis*

RÉCIT   Flûte harmonique, Bourdon, Gambe, Voix céleste
G^d-ORGUE   Flûte harmonique & Bourdon
PÉDALE   Bourdon de 16

CAMILLE SAINT-SAËNS
1835–1921

Transcribed by Louis Courtade

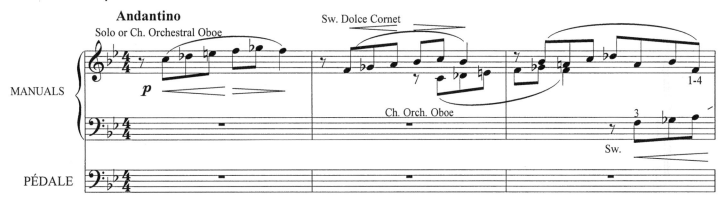

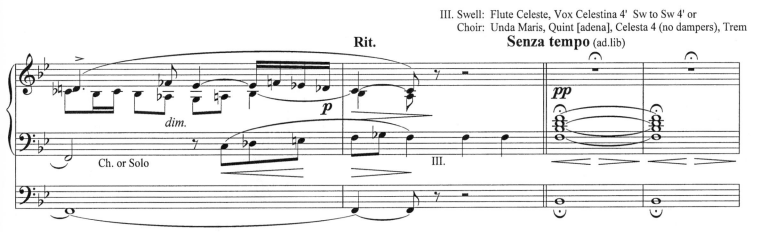

Solo 8' Heckelphone, Trem. or Orch. Oboe

THE SWAN

LE CYGNE

from *The Carnival of the Animals*

RÉCIT   Bourdon, Flûte de 8 et Trompette (ou Basson). Boîte fermée.
POSITIF   Flûte et Salicional de 8
G^d-ORGUE   Bourdon et Flûte de 8. Récit accouplé.
PÉDALE   Soubasse de 16, Bourdon et Violoncelle de 8

CAMILLE SAINT-SAËNS
1835–1921

Transcribed by Alexandre Guilmant

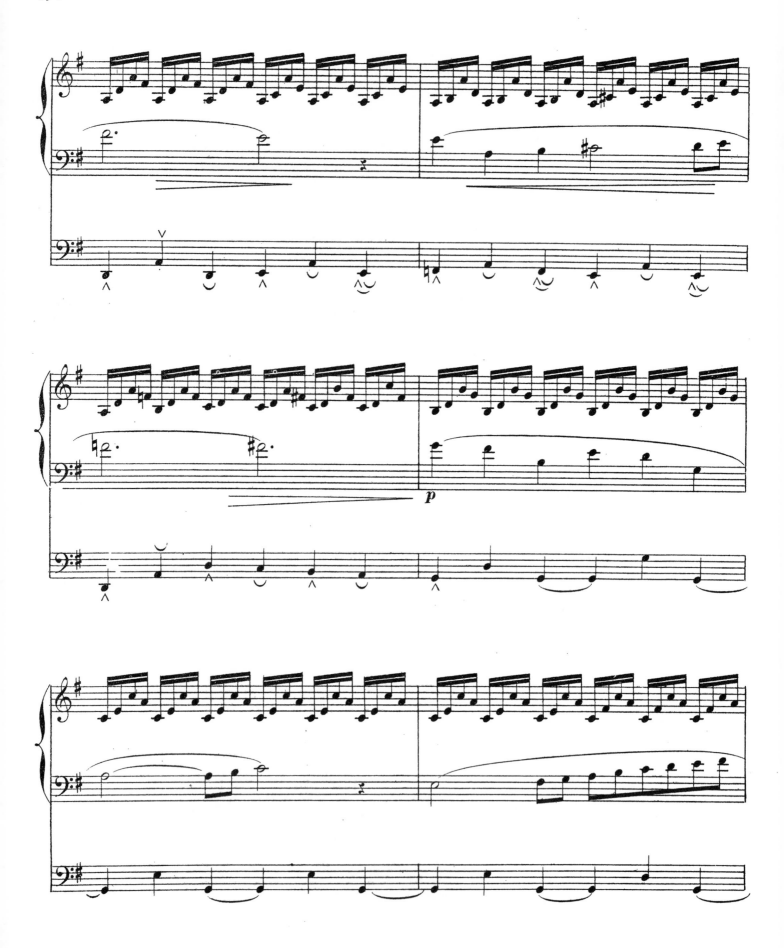

DANCE OF THE SUGAR PLUM FAIRY

from *The Nutcracker Suite,* Op. 71a

Sw. Strings and Gedeckt
Gt. Open Diapasons 16' & 8'
Ch. Flutes 8' – 4' – 2' (Celesta ad lib.)
Ped. Bourdon 16' – 8' Ch. to Ped.

PETER ILYITCH TCHAIKOVSKY
(1840-1893)

Arranged by Gordon Balch Nevin

Celesta alone, where possible, otherwise - 2´ off

DANSE ARABE

from *The Nutcracker Suite,* Op. 71a

Sw.   Strings and Gedeckt
Gt.   Erzähler, or soft 8'
Ch.   Clarinet
Ped. Bourdon & Violone Uncoupled

Arranged by Gordon Balch Nevin

PETER ILYITCH TCHAIKOVSKY
(1840-1893)

*Eight measures were omitted; they may be restored by inserting measures 5 through 12 at this point.

DANCE OF THE REED PIPES

from *The Nutcracker Suite,* Op. 71a

Sw. Flutes 8' – 4' – 2' with trem.
Gt. Gross Flute
Ch. Cor Anglais, or Clarinet
Ped. Bourdon 16' – 8' Sw. to Ped.

PETER ILYITCH TCHAIKOVSKY
(1840-1893)

Arranged by Gordon Balch Nevin

ANGÉLUS

from *Scènes pittoresques*

Gt. Chimes (or 8' stop)
Sw. 8' & 4', with Oboe
Ch. Voix Celestes
Ped. 16' & 8' *p*

JULES MASSENET
1842–1912

Arranged by Humphrey J. Stewart

à Paul Dukas

PRELUDE TO *THE BLESSED DAMOZEL*

LA DAMOISELLE ÉLUE

Swell: Aeoline and Unda Maris
Great: Erzähler 8' (or Gemshorn 8')
Choir: Celesta or Harp 8' pitch
Solo: Orchestral Oboe
Echo: Flute 4' or Quintadena
Pedal: no registers; Sw. to Ped. only

CLAUDE DEBUSSY
1862–1918

Transcribed by Palmer Christian

Sw: *pp* Unda Maris (or Flute Céleste)

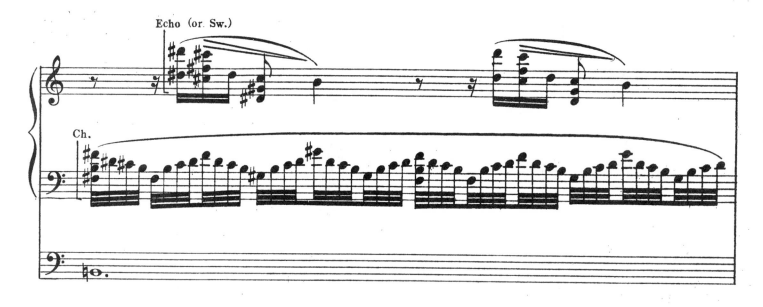

Echo (or. Sw.)

Ch.

ppp

Ch.